Through the Ups and Downs His Love is Found

Written by Melissa Norton ✦ Illustrated by Daniel Norton

First Printing: 2019

ISBN: 978-1-7335922-0-8

Mustard Seed™
PUBLISHING

www.mustardseedpublishing.com

✦ 10% of all profits from this book are donated to
single parents to provide support in times of need.

✦ ✦
✦

This book was created with love for you!
In sharing our testimony we hope to create
a stillness between parent and child;
fixing your hearts and minds on
the unchanging love of Jesus Christ
in the midst of this ever-changing world.
It's our prayer to bring love, hope,
and comfort to others who are
on a similar journey.

All of a sudden it was us...
just mommy, brother, and me.

All of a sudden it was us...
just me and daddy.

Deuteronomy 31:8

I was confused. I felt sad. Sometimes my sad would turn into MAD! No matter how hard I tried, sometimes I just wanted to hide.

I didn't know why I felt I could cry. As daddy held me I would try to hide it. I would rest on his shoulder and stay very quiet.

1 Peter 5:7

So much was changing I didn't understand why...??? My mommy told me with a tear in her eye, "In life there will be change, many ups and downs, but through it all God's love is found. Some change brings joy, some will bring pain, but the love of God remains the same."

All that was changing a new house, no more pets. I just didn't know what would happen next...??? Daddy reminded me that in God's love we must rest and that His plans for us are the very best.

Jeremiah 29:11

The days went by, sometimes I would still cry, so Mommy would take us to the beach to play in the warm sand. At the beach is where we felt Jesus holding our hand.

As the days passed we began to cheer up, but there still were times my eyes would tear up. Daddy would take me to the beach where we would laugh and play. At the beach is where we felt Jesus take the sad away.

Matthew 11:28-30

More time passed day by day, I started to feel the sad go away. We enjoyed life together one day at a time, while playing outside God's wonders we'd find. Flying blue bugs, bees, butterflies, tag, T-ball or a game of catch, but the giant bubbles were always the best!

More days went by just daddy and I. I no longer felt the need to cry. Our days were spent no one like the other. We would find parks, watch the sunset, and enjoy one another. My favorite time was spent drawing with daddy in the café, I started to feel in my heart that it would all be okay.

Psalms 147:3

Then one day I met a little girl who was kind as can be. Mommy told me she was the same age as me! Her name was Audrey. She was so shy sitting there with her soft brown curly hair. We just sat on the swing and didn't say a thing.

Then one day as I was sitting on a swing, I met a boy named Noah and it changed everything! He sat next to me with his eyes bright blue, but all he could do was look down at his shoe.

Matthew 18:3

I jumped off the swing and looked up to see Audrey's dad standing there. He waived at me and said, "Hey there! My name is Daniel," with his voice full of care.

I looked over to see Noah's brother Dexter playing in the sand. That's when I met their mommy as she reached down for his hand. She said her name was Melissa or Missy, whichever I prefer. So I called her Melissy, because I wasn't quite sure.

Job 8:7

We didn't know what God had in store as we started to see Daniel and Audrey more and more. Oh what joy they would bring after that day we met on the swing. Our adventure of three was becoming an adventure of five. In the time spent together we felt so alive. Sharing with them our love for camping with the bears, blue jays and deer. I am so thankful Jesus led us here.

Since that day sitting on the swing, oh the adventure their love would bring. Camping, kayaking, laughter and play, I am ever so thankful for that day. Our days were no longer just daddy and me, I am so happy God sent us these three.

Proverbs 3:5-6

On this special day I knew in Daniel's love we could confide. He had made our mommy his bride! A step-dad! A sister! It was no longer us three. God pieced together a beautiful family.

Then on this special day, our dresses matching white, I knew her love would forever hold me tight. A step-mommy! Two brothers! I was overwhelmed with love. A beautiful gift sent from our Father above.

Ecclesiastes 3:11

Now for us it's picnics, pizza Fridays, and paper airplanes that soar. We continue to look forward to what God has in store. Unexplainable joy and lots of laughter — this is our family's happily ever after.

Our life changed so beautifully for it's in God we place
our trust. We know there are others who have felt like us.
Trust in the Lord. He will carry you through;
the ups and downs and all that you do.

www.ingramcontent.com/pod-product-compliance
Lightning Source LLC
Chambersburg PA
CBHW060816090426
42737CB00002B/78

9781733592208